AI FOR CREATIVES

A GUIDE FOR ARTISTS, MUSICIANS, AND WRITERS

AI FOR CREATIVES

AI FOR CREATIVES:

A GUIDE FOR ARTISTS, MUSICIANS, AND WRITERS

AI FOR CREATIVES

AI FOR CREATIVES

COPYRIGHT

All rights reserved. © 2024 AMBW Press

No part of this book may be reproduced, stored in a retrieval system, or transmitted in any form or by any means, electronic, mechanical, photocopying, recording, or otherwise, without the written permission of the publisher/writer.

The views expressed in this work are solely those of the author and do not necessarily reflect the views of any other individual or entity.

Artwork: AI-Generated
Publisher: AMBW Press
AMBWPress@yahoo.com

AI FOR CREATIVES

AI FOR CREATIVES

TABLE OF CONTENTS

BRIEF SUMMARY

GLOSSARY

INTRODUCTION

CHAPTER 1

CHAPTER 2

CHAPTER 3

CHAPTER 4

CHAPTER 5

CHAPTER 6

CHAPTER 7

CHAPTER 8

CHAPTER 9

CHAPTER 10

CHAPTER 11

CHAPTER 12

CONCLUSION

APPENDIX

AI FOR CREATIVES

AI FOR CREATIVES

BRIEF SUMMARY

Partner with AI to Unleash Your Inner Mastermind

Imagine a future where your artistic muse is a digital whiz, a partner in creative crime-fighting. That's the world this book explores! We delve into the exciting possibilities of AI, not as a replacement for human creativity but as a supercharged sidekick.

Think email-assassinating AI freeing you to focus on crafting masterpieces or AI composers crafting music that adapts to the mood of the audience. We explore the potential pitfalls, like AI perpetuating hidden biases, and how to navigate the ethical landscape responsibly.

But most importantly, this book is a celebration of the future of creativity. It's a world where AI and human artists join forces to push boundaries, dream up fantastical creatures, and tell stories in revolutionary ways. So, grab your metaphorical paintbrush and get ready to co-create the future of art with your trusty AI partner!

AI FOR CREATIVES

AI FOR CREATIVES

GLOSSARY

Key Terms Related to AI and Creative Processes:

AI (Artificial Intelligence): The ability of machines to mimic cognitive functions that humans associate with other human mental activities, such as learning and problem-solving. In the context of creativity, AI refers to algorithms trained on vast amounts of data to perform tasks like generating creative text formats, composing music, or creating images.

Machine Learning: A type of AI where algorithms learn and improve without being explicitly programmed. Machine learning algorithms used in creative processes are often trained on massive datasets of creative works, like paintings, musical pieces, or written text.

Deep Learning: A subfield of machine learning inspired by the structure and function of the human brain. Deep learning algorithms use artificial neural networks to process information and learn from data. These are often employed in AI tools for generating creative text formats, creating realistic images, or composing music.

Natural Language Processing (NLP): A subfield of AI concerned with the interaction between computers and human language. NLP techniques are used in AI writing assistants to understand the context and intent of a user's request and generate creative text formats that are grammatically sound and stylistically appropriate.

Generative AI: A type of AI that can create new and original content, such as images, text, or music. Generative AI models are often used in creative tools to help artists and writers overcome creative roadblocks or explore new artistic directions.

Bias: A prejudice or preconceived notion that can be reflected in the results of an AI model. Bias can creep into AI creative tools if the data they are trained on is biased. For example, an AI image generator trained on a dataset of photos that primarily depicts people with a certain skin tone might struggle to generate realistic images of people with different skin tones.

Algorithmic Transparency: The ability to understand how an AI model arrives at its outputs. In the context of creative processes, algorithmic transparency is important for ensuring that AI tools are not perpetuating biases or producing unexpected or undesirable results.

AI Assistant: A software program that uses AI to automate tasks, provide information, or complete creative requests. AI assistants for creative processes can help with tasks like generating new ideas, streamlining workflows, or improving the quality of creative outputs.

AI FOR CREATIVES

Co-creation: A collaborative process where humans and AI work together to create something new. In the context of art and creativity, co-creation can involve using AI tools to generate ideas, refine concepts, or create different variations of a work in progress.

AI FOR CREATIVES

# INTRODUCTION

Da Vinci's Digital Apprentice: How AI is Revolutionizing Art

Remember those clunky robots from sci-fi movies, programmed to conquer and control? Forget that. Artificial intelligence (AI) has shed its villainous reputation and is here to be your creative partner-in-crime, not your robotic overlord.

Those worried that AI will steal their artistic mojo can breathe easily. Think of AI as that missing tool in your toolbox – the one that unlocks a hidden world of inspiration, streamlines your workflow like a boss, and blasts past creative roadblocks faster than you can say, "Eureka!"

This book is your personal guide to wielding the power of AI. Whether you're a painter wrestling with a blank canvas, a musician yearning for a fresh melody, or a writer facing a stubborn case of writer's block, AI is here to be your secret weapon. We'll delve into the coolest AI tools for artists, musicians, and writers, showing you how to use them to spark ideas, collaborate on projects, and conquer your creative goals.

So, ditch the fear and grab your metaphorical paintbrush (or microphone, or keyboard) – it's time to unleash your inner Da Vinci with the help of AI!

AI FOR CREATIVES

CHAPTER 1

Demystifying the Muse Machine:
What AI Really Is (and Isn't) for Creatives

Have you ever stared at a blank canvas, a silent instrument, or a blinking cursor, feeling like your creativity has packed its bags and gone on a permanent vacation? Is your muse MIA, replaced by a persistent case of "been-there-done-that" syndrome? Fear not, fellow artist, musician, or writer! In this chapter, we'll be your own personal Lewis Carroll, tumbling down the rabbit hole of Artificial Intelligence (AI) and showing you exactly what this enigmatic technology can (and can't) do to reignite your creative fire.

Now, before you start picturing robots composing symphonies or churning out award-winning novels, let's dispel some myths. AI isn't some sentient being ready to steal your artistic thunder. It's more like a fantastical toolbox overflowing with incredible gadgets designed to supercharge your creative process. Imagine a brainstorming partner on steroids, tossing out wild ideas and unexpected prompts to get those creative juices flowing like a burst dam.

We'll delve into the fascinating world of AI, unpacking its capabilities like a magician revealing their secret tricks. You'll discover how AI can be your muse machine, sparking inspiration and helping you break free from

AI FOR CREATIVES

creative ruts. We'll explore how it can generate new ideas, analyze vast amounts of data to inform your work, and even collaborate with you on projects – think of it as your own personal artistic wingman!

But here's the thing: AI isn't here to replace you. It's here to empower you. It can't replicate the raw human emotion poured into a painting, the soul woven into a melody, or the unique voice that shapes a story. AI is a powerful tool, but it's still just a tool. The magic, the heart, the true essence of your creative vision – that all comes from you.

So, cast aside any anxieties and grab your metaphorical paintbrush (or microphone or keyboard). It's time to meet your new AI muse machine and embark on a creative adventure unlike any other! Buckle up because we're about to unlock a treasure trove of possibilities waiting to transform your artistic journey.

AI FOR CREATIVES

AI FOR CREATIVES

CHAPTER 2

**The AI Candy Store:
A Glimpse into the Wild World of Creative AI Tools**

Cast aside your preconceived notions of dusty computer labs and whirring machines because the landscape of creative AI tools is more like a Willy Wonka fever dream come to life! Forget chocolate rivers and everlasting gobstoppers – here, the shelves overflow with fantastical tools designed to ignite your artistic spark. Buckle up, fellow creative explorer, because we're about to embark on a whirlwind tour through this wonderland.

First stop: The Image Alchemist's Alley! Here, AI transforms into your personal genie, conjuring visual landscapes that would make even the most seasoned artist gape in awe. Feeling like your painting is stuck in a creative cul-de-sac? With a few clicks of the mouse, AI can whisk you away to a fantastical alien world bathed in bioluminescent flora or a photorealistic cityscape slick with neon rain. Need a cast of unforgettable characters for your graphic novel? Let AI be your character design sketchpad, churning out a variety of options, each more intriguing and unique than the last.

Next, we venture into the Melody Maker's Workshop, a symphony of possibilities conducted by AI. Here, your muse takes the form of a digital maestro, whipping up catchy hooks that burrow into your earworms or

AI FOR CREATIVES

weaving intricate orchestral pieces that perfectly capture the emotional depth of your musical vision. Stuck on a writer's block for your next song's lyrics? No problem! AI morphs into your brainstorming buddy, tossing out unexpected rhymes, thematic twists, and lyrical turns that will get those creative gears churning faster than a runaway metronome.

But hold on tight because the adventure doesn't stop there! We haven't even reached the Writer's Wordsmithy, a haven overflowing with AI assistants that function as your own personal editor and brainstorming partner rolled into one. Need help crafting the perfect sentence to elevate your prose or overcoming a stubborn case of writer's block that's clinging to your manuscript like a particularly tenacious barnacle? AI can be your knight in shining armor, tossing out creative prompts that spark inspiration, analyzing your writing style to suggest alternative phrasing, and even fact-checking your work with the meticulousness of a digital librarian.

Remember, this is just a glimpse into the treasure trove of AI tools at your disposal. We'll delve deeper into each one, helping you identify the perfect companions for your creative journey, whether you're a painter yearning for a splash of inspiration, a musician seeking a fresh melody, or a writer fighting the blank page blues. So, unleash your inner Willy Wonka and get ready to explore the wonders of the AI candy store for creatives! The key to unlocking a world of artistic possibilities awaits.

AI FOR CREATIVES

AI FOR CREATIVES

CHAPTER 3

Navigating the AI Art Bazaar:
Picking the Perfect Tool for Your Creative Needs

Welcome back, intrepid creative explorer! You've just glimpsed the dazzling array of AI tools at your disposal, and your mind is likely buzzing with a million possibilities. But hold your metaphorical paintbrushes, tap shoes, or quills – before you embark on a digital shopping spree that would make even Kim Kardashian jealous, let's navigate the bustling AI Art Bazaar and find the perfect tools for your unique creative vision.

Think of it like stepping into a fantastical art supply store overflowing with every imaginable tool – from shimmering watercolors to colossal house-painting brushes. Just like you wouldn't grab that giant brush for a delicate watercolor masterpiece, the key to unlocking the full potential of AI lies in choosing the tools that perfectly complement your creative style and skill level.

Are you a seasoned painter facing a stubborn case of creative block or a budding musician yearning for a melody muse? Do you crave an AI assistant that throws wild, abstract ideas at the wall like a digital Jackson Pollock or a meticulous tool for fine-tuning details with the precision of a Swiss watchmaker?

AI FOR CREATIVES

Fear not, fellow creative! We'll equip you with a handy map to navigate the AI Art Bazaar. We'll explore the diverse tool categories, from the "Idea Spark Generator" (perfect for igniting your imagination and blasting past creative roadblocks) to the "Grammar Guru" (your digital editor in shining armor, ready to polish your prose until it gleams). We'll even decipher the often-confusing hieroglyphics of features and functionalities, ensuring you don't get lost in a labyrinth of technical jargon that would make a sphinx blush.

Remember, the best AI tool isn't a one-size-fits-all solution. It's the one that seamlessly integrates into your existing workflow and empowers you to express your unique artistic voice. By the end of this chapter, you'll be a master navigator of the AI Art Bazaar, able to identify the perfect AI gems that will elevate your creative process and transform your artistic vision into a breathtaking masterpiece. So, grab your metaphorical shopping basket, and let's get ready to find the tools that will unlock a world of creative possibilities and propel you toward artistic nirvana!

AI FOR CREATIVES

AI FOR CREATIVES

CHAPTER 4

Slaying the Blank Page Beast: How AI Can Spark Wild Ideas (and Banish Creative Block Forever)

The dreaded blank page. It sits there, a mocking white expanse, a creative black hole that seems to gobble up all your inspiration and leave you feeling like a deflated balloon. Fear not, fellow artist, musician, and writer! In this chapter, we'll unveil the secret weapon in your arsenal: AI, the ultimate blank page beast slayer, and your personal muse on steroids.

Forget staring at that empty canvas or blinking cursor until your eyeballs feel like overripe blueberries. AI is here to be your artistic defibrillator, shocking your creative heart back to life with a jolt of electrifying inspiration. We'll delve into a treasure trove of techniques to use AI as your personal idea spark generator, no matter your artistic discipline.

For the Visually Inclined:
- **Random Inspiration Roulette:** Feeling like your painting is trapped in a creative cul-de-sac? Let AI spin the wheel of artistic chance! We'll show you how to use AI image generators to create random prompts – swirling galaxies where stars waltz, fantastical creatures with iridescent scales, or dreamlike landscapes bathed in the

light of three moons. These unexpected visual springboards will ignite your imagination and send your creativity down wild, exhilarating avenues.

- **Style Mashup Mastermind:** Is your artistic style feeling a bit stale? Let AI be your artistic remix maestro! We'll explore how to use AI to analyze the works of your favorite artists (think Van Gogh meets Monet, or a sprinkle of Picasso's whimsy in your next portrait). This cross-pollination of styles can spark unexpected ideas and help you break free from creative ruts, breathing new life into your artistic vision.

For the Musically Minded:
- **Genre-Bending Remixes:** Is your song stuck in a predictable melody loop? Let AI be your musical alchemist! We'll delve into using AI tools to take your existing melody and transform it into different genres. Imagine a folksy ballad turned into a head-banging rock anthem that would make mosh pits erupt or a melancholic piano piece morphed into an upbeat electronic dance track guaranteed to get toes tapping. These unexpected genre twists can open up a world of creative possibilities and help you discover hidden dimensions within your music.

- **Unexpected Instrumentation Playground:** Feeling limited by your usual instruments? Let AI be your sonic explorer! We'll show you how to use AI to experiment with different instruments and soundscapes. Imagine a violin solo transformed into a hauntingly beautiful cello melody or a guitar riff given a whole new life with the addition of traditional Chinese flutes. These unexpected sonic combinations can add depth and texture to your music, taking your listeners on a truly unique auditory journey.

For the Word Wielders:

- **Story Starter Springboard:** Does your novel manuscript feel like it's going nowhere fast? Let AI be your plot twist mastermind! We'll show you how to use AI writing prompts to generate unexpected story ideas, character backstories that go deeper than a Mariana Trench, or even plot twists that will leave you gasping and itching to get back to writing. Imagine your protagonist waking up to discover they can talk to animals or a seemingly ordinary object, becoming the key to unlocking a hidden world – these AI-powered prompts can send your story in thrilling new directions and keep your readers on the edge of their seats.

- **Character Quirks and Dialogue Doctor:** Are your characters feeling a bit one-dimensional? Let AI be your character development coach! We'll explore how to use AI to generate random character quirks, personality traits, or even dialogue snippets that can breathe life into your characters and make them leap off the page. Imagine a timid librarian with a secret passion for skydiving or a grumpy detective with a surprising love for baking – these unexpected details can make your characters truly unforgettable and add depth to your narrative.

Remember, AI isn't here to replace your creativity; it's here to supercharge it. By the end of this chapter, you'll be a master of using AI to overcome creative block, generate fresh ideas that will make your work sing, and banish the blank page beast to the depths of creative oblivion. So, grab your metaphorical paintbrush, microphone, or keyboard, and let's get ready to unleash a torrent of creativity fueled by the power of AI!

AI FOR CREATIVES

AI FOR CREATIVES

CHAPTER 5

The AI Muse Brigade:
How You and AI Can Co-Create Like Rockstars
(or Renaissance Masters)

Forget the solitary artist toiling away in a garret fueled by angst and flickering candlelight. The future of creativity is collaborative, and AI is here to be your artistic wingman, your musical co-conspirator, and your literary dream team. In this chapter, we'll smash the stereotype of the lonely creator and delve into the exciting world of AI-powered collaboration. Imagine your artistic muse not just visiting occasionally but becoming your permanent partner-in-crime, helping you bring your vision to life in ways you never dreamed possible.

For the Visually Inclined:
- **AI, Your Master Sketch Artist:** Stuck on a specific element in your painting? Let AI be your digital Michelangelo! We'll show you how to use AI to generate a multitude of variations – a character's pose captured from every angle, a building's architectural details explored in meticulous detail, or a fantastical creature's anatomy rendered with scientific precision. Think of it as having a tireless sketch artist at your disposal, churning out endless variations until you find the perfect visual element to complete

your masterpiece. No more staring at a blank canvas, paralyzed by indecision – AI becomes your brainstorming partner, helping you explore possibilities and refine your vision.

- **The Color Palette Alchemist:** Feeling uninspired by your usual color choices? Let AI be your chromatic compass! We'll show you how to use AI to generate unique color palettes based on emotions, historical periods, or even famous paintings. Imagine a portrait bathed in the ethereal glow of a Monet sunrise or a landscape bursting with the vibrant hues of a Van Gogh masterpiece. These unexpected color combinations can add a whole new dimension to your artwork and push your creative boundaries. Think of AI as your artistic color consultant, helping you break free from predictable palettes and discover hidden depths of emotion and meaning within your work.

For the Musically Minded:
- **The AI Lyrical Brainstorm Buddy:** Hit a wall with your song lyrics? Let AI be your rhyme-slinging sidekick! We'll explore how to use AI to generate lyric suggestions, rhyming partners that would make Eminem jealous, or even thematic twists to take your song in unexpected directions. Imagine collaborating with a tireless lyricist who throws out wild ideas, helping you craft catchy hooks and verses that will have your audience

singing along. Brainstorming with AI isn't about replacing your creativity; it's about supercharging it, sparking new ideas, and helping you refine your message with unexpected turns of phrase.

- **The AI Melody Machine:** Feeling creatively stagnant with your melody? Let AI be your sonic sparring partner! We'll show you how to use AI to generate musical samples that push your boundaries, counter-melodies that add depth and texture, or even variations on your existing theme that take your song in exciting new directions. Think of it as having a musical mastermind by your side, offering fresh sonic ideas and helping you explore new musical landscapes within your song. No more writer's block for melodies – AI becomes your creative sounding board, helping you experiment and discover hidden potential within your music.

For the Word Wielders:
- **The AI Story Architect:** Does your plot feel like it's meandering aimlessly? Let AI be your narrative compass! We'll explore how to use AI to generate plot points that will keep your readers on the edge of their seats, character motivations that add depth and complexity, or even world-building details to flesh out your fictional universe. Imagine brainstorming with a digital architect who helps you map out unexpected

twists, surprising character arcs, or intriguing details about your fictional world. AI isn't here to write your story for you; it's here to be your creative confidante, helping you explore possibilities and refine your narrative structure.

- **The AI Dialogue Doctor:** Are your characters' conversations getting a bit stale? Let AI be your dialogue coach! We'll show you how to use AI to generate realistic dialogue snippets, witty banter that would make Oscar Wilde blush, or unexpected turns of phrase that will make your characters come alive on the page. Imagine having a dialogue consultant at your fingertips, helping you craft conversations that crackle with wit, tension, or emotional depth. AI becomes your secret weapon for character development, ensuring your characters are not just cardboard cutouts but multi-dimensional beings with believable voices and personalities.

Remember, AI isn't here to take over your creative vision; it's here to augment it. By the end of this chapter, you'll be a master collaborator, wielding AI as your secret weapon to co-create groundbreaking works of art, music, and literature. So, grab your metaphorical paintbrush, microphone, or keyboard, and get ready to embark on a creative journey with your new AI muse.

AI FOR CREATIVES

AI FOR CREATIVES

CHAPTER 6

Building Worlds Beyond Your Wildest Dreams: How AI Can Be Your Architect and Artist

Have you ever dreamt of crafting a fictional world so immersive that your readers feel the dragon smoke sting their nostrils or hear the rhythmic thrumming of alien music pulse through the bustling marketplace of a forgotten civilization? Buckle up, wordsmiths and visual architects alike, because AI is here to be your world-building architect and artist, helping you forge fantastical landscapes that would make J.R.R. Tolkien and Frank Frazetta do a double-take!

For the Word Wielders:

- **AI, Your Descriptive Detail Dynamo:** Feeling like your world descriptions are a bit...lackluster? Let AI be your thesaurus on steroids! We'll show you how to use AI to generate vivid descriptions that would make even the most seasoned travel writer envious. Imagine having a bottomless well of sensory details at your fingertips – the acrid tang of volcanic fumes mingling with the sweet, heady scent of bioluminescent flora in an alien jungle, the rhythmic crunch of footsteps on ancient, moss-covered cobblestones, the cacophony of a bustling marketplace filled with exotic creatures hawking their wares in a language that sings like wind chimes. AI becomes your descriptive paintbrush, helping you paint a picture with words that will transport your readers right into the heart of your fictional world, leaving them breathless with its immersive detail.

- **The AI Character Creation Crucible:** Need a cast of characters as unforgettable as Arya Stark or Han Solo? Let AI be your character foundry! We'll delve into using AI to generate character backstories that are as rich and complex as a Tolkienian family tree, personalities that leap off the page and grab your readers by the throat, and even physical descriptions that go beyond the tired tropes of the brooding hero or the damsel in distress. Imagine fleshing out your world with a stoic warrior princess with a hidden love for poetry and a cybernetic arm that hums with dormant power, a wisecracking mechanic with a cybernetic eye that can see through walls and a heart full of loyalty, or a grumpy troll with a love for baking exquisite pastries and a surprising knowledge of ancient lore. AI becomes your character sculptor, helping you create a diverse and engaging cast that will populate your world and keep your readers turning the pages long into the night.

For the Visually Inclined:
- **The AI Concept Art Catalyst:** Stuck visualizing that fantastical creature or high-tech gadget? Let

AI FOR CREATIVES

AI be your artistic muse on overdrive! We'll explore how to use AI to generate concept art based on your descriptions, no matter how strange or wonderful. Imagine conjuring up a majestic griffin with iridescent feathers that shimmer like opals and razor-sharp claws that could rend steel, a sleek spaceship that wouldn't look out of place in a Star Wars movie but boasts a bioluminescent hull that pulses with an otherworldly glow, or a bustling marketplace filled with fantastical creatures from all corners of your imagination – from hulking, six-armed warriors to mischievous imps with eyes that sparkle with mischief. AI becomes your visual brainstorming partner, helping you translate your ideas into stunning visuals that will serve as a springboard for your artwork, breathing life into your fictional world before you even put brush to canvas.

- **The AI Environment Architect:** Need help designing the perfect landscape for your painting or graphic novel? Let AI be your digital landscape architect with a boundless imagination! We'll show you how to use AI to generate detailed environments that would make even the most seasoned landscape painter blush. Think sprawling alien jungles teeming with bioluminescent flora that casts an ethereal glow on the moss-covered ruins of a forgotten civilization, ancient underwater cities built on the backs of giant sea turtles that migrate across vast, bioluminescent oceans, or windswept deserts under a crimson sun where nomadic tribes ride colossal sandworms. Imagine having a limitless library of landscapes at your disposal, each one as unique and breathtaking as the last. AI becomes your world-building paintbrush, helping you create stunning backdrops that will bring your fictional universe to life in a way that is both visually captivating and narratively rich.

Remember, AI isn't here to replace your imagination; it's here to supercharge it. By the end of this chapter, you'll be a master world-builder, wielding AI as your secret weapon to craft fictional landscapes that are as rich and detailed as your wildest dreams. So, grab your metaphorical pen, paintbrush, or stylus, and get ready to embark on a journey of epic world-building fueled by the power of AI! Let your imagination soar and watch as AI helps you transform your creative vision into a reality that will leave your readers and viewers breathless.

AI FOR CREATIVES

AI FOR CREATIVES

CHAPTER 7

Conquering the Research Rabbit Hole: How AI Can Be Your Super-Powered Research Assistant and Organizational Guru

Ever felt like researching your historical novel has become a nightmarish descent into a dusty library labyrinth filled with cobweb-laden tomes and overflowing digital archives? Or maybe your musical inspiration board resembles the aftermath of a confetti explosion in a music store, a chaotic jumble of scribbled notes, half-formed melodies, and dog-eared sheet music? Fear not, fellow creatives! In this chapter, we'll unveil AI, your secret weapon for conquering research and organization woes. Think of it as transforming yourself from a lone explorer hacking your way through the research jungle to Indiana Jones, armed with a cutting-edge AI machete and a trusty digital map.

For the Word Wielders:
- **The AI Research Rabbit Hole Tamer:** Drowning in a sea of historical documents or scientific studies that would make even the Library of Congress blush? Let AI be your research lifeguard, throwing you a virtual lifeline! We'll show you how to use AI to sift through mountains of information faster than a hummingbird can sip nectar, identifying the most relevant sources and even extracting key facts,

quotes, and statistics to save you precious time. Imagine having a tireless research assistant with superhuman reading comprehension who can scan through libraries faster than you can say "bibliography," surfacing the most valuable nuggets of information to fuel your writing. No more endless hours spent wading through irrelevant articles – AI becomes your research filter, ensuring you only encounter the information that truly matters for your masterpiece.

- **The AI Citation Slayer:** Does the thought of formatting citations in different styles (MLA, APA, Chicago – the list goes on!) make you want to hurl your laptop into the nearest volcano? Let AI be your citation superhero, swooping in to save the day! We'll explore how to use AI to automatically generate citations in various styles, transforming your messy reference list into a perfectly formatted masterpiece. Imagine having a citation magician at your fingertips, waving a metaphorical wand, and banishing the formatting gremlins that plague writers everywhere. No more late nights spent wrestling with style guides – AI becomes your citation guardian angel, ensuring your bibliography is as flawless as your prose.

For the Musically Minded:

AI FOR CREATIVES

- **The AI Genre Guru:** Feeling lost in the vast ocean of musical styles and influences, adrift without a sonic compass? Let AI be your musical lighthouse, guiding you through the musical landscape! We'll show you how to use AI to analyze existing music in different genres, identify key characteristics like tempo, instrumentation, and chord progressions, and even generate soundscapes that capture the essence of a particular style. Imagine having a musical historian and trendspotter on your side, helping you understand the DNA of different genres. Think of AI as your portal to a vast sonic library, allowing you to draw inspiration from the masters and inject fresh influences into your own music.

- **The AI Song Organization Maestro:** Is your musical inspiration board overflowing with chaotic scribbles, half-formed melodies, and stray guitar picks like a musician's warzone? Let AI be your organizational maestro, transforming your creative chaos into a symphony of order! We'll delve into using AI to categorize your musical ideas by genre, mood, or theme and even suggest ways to connect them into cohesive song structures. Imagine having a digital filing cabinet for your musical ideas, where everything is meticulously categorized and easily accessible. No more lost melodies or forgotten riffs – AI becomes your musical librarian, ensuring every

AI FOR CREATIVES

spark of inspiration is documented and readily available to be revisited and refined into a masterpiece.

Remember, AI isn't here to replace your critical thinking or creativity; it's here to streamline your workflow and empower you to focus on what you do best – creating! By the end of this chapter, you'll be a master of using AI to conquer research rabbit holes, tame organizational chaos, and transform yourself into a productivity powerhouse. So, grab your metaphorical pen and notebook or your trusty musical instrument, and get ready to unleash your creative potential with the help of your AI research assistant and organizational guru! Let AI become your secret weapon and watch as you navigate the creative landscape with newfound confidence and efficiency.

AI FOR CREATIVES

AI FOR CREATIVES

CHAPTER 8

From Drafts to Diamonds:
How AI Can Be Your Editing Eagle Eye and Polishing Partner

Staring at your manuscript, littered with typos and plot holes bigger than a dragon's appetite? Feeling like your prose could use a good shine, but a human editor's fees are enough to make your wallet weep? Worry not, wordsmiths! In this chapter, we'll unveil AI, your secret weapon for transforming your rough drafts into polished gems. Imagine the satisfaction of holding your finished novel, a testament to your creativity and the invaluable assistance of your AI partner.

AI, Your Editing Eagle Eye:
- **The Grammar Gremlin Slayer:** Dreading another round of comma hunts and verb tense battles? Let AI be your grammar swat team! We'll show you how to use AI to identify and eradicate those pesky grammar gremlins – misplaced commas that turn a thrilling chase scene into a picnic ("Fleeing the guards, the princess tripped, tumbling head over heels," versus the grammatically correct, "Fleeing the guards, the princess tripped, tumbling head over heels."), rogue apostrophes that make your characters sound like pirates who never learned the rules of the high seas ("Let's explore this creepy

basement!" versus the shudder-inducingly correct, "Let's explore this creepy basement!"), and subject-verb agreement issues that make your editor twitch ("The group of adventurers waded cautiously through the swamp," not, "The group of adventurers waded cautiously through the swamps."). Imagine having a tireless grammar watchdog by your side, scanning your manuscript with laser focus and highlighting every error that might make your English teacher cry. With AI's help, you can focus on the bigger picture of your story, leaving the nitty-gritty grammar work to your digital assistant.

- **The Plot Hole Plugger:** Is your plot riddled with holes bigger than Swiss cheese? Let AI be your narrative compass! We'll explore how to use AI to analyze your story structure, identify inconsistencies, and even suggest ways to plug those pesky plot holes that could leave your readers scratching their heads. Imagine having a digital story architect on your team, dissecting your plot and offering suggestions for smoother transitions – perhaps a missing scene that explains why the villain suddenly switched sides or stronger character motivations – and a more satisfying climax. With AI's help, you can ensure your story flows like a mighty river, captivating your readers from the first page to the last.

AI, Your Polishing Partner:

AI FOR CREATIVES

- **The Word Choice Wizard:** Feeling like your vocabulary is stuck on repeat, relying on the same tired adjectives and adverbs? Let AI be your thesaurus on overdrive! We'll show you how to use AI to identify overused words and suggest more nuanced alternatives that will add depth and richness to your prose. Imagine having a word wizard at your fingertips, conjuring up a cornucopia of synonyms that will elevate your writing from good to great. Instead of describing a character's eyes as simply "blue," AI might suggest "sapphire," "cerulean," or even "storm-cloud gray," depending on the desired effect. With AI's help, you can banish bland vocabulary and paint your story with the vibrant colors of language, making your characters and settings come alive in the reader's mind.

- **The Pacing Pro:** Is your story dragging in some spots and sprinting in others, leaving your readers confused and breathless? Let AI be your pacing metronome! We'll delve into using AI to analyze the flow of your narrative and identify areas that might be bogging down the pace or rushing your readers. Imagine having a digital editor with a keen sense of rhythm, helping you ensure your story unfolds at a pace that keeps your readers engaged and eager to turn the page. With AI's guidance, you can fine-tune the pacing of your story, creating a reading experience that is both thrilling and satisfying. Perhaps AI will suggest adding a scene to build suspense before a big reveal or trimming down overly descriptive passages that slow down the narrative momentum.

Remember, AI isn't here to replace your own editorial judgment; it's here to be your partner in crime. By the end of this chapter, you'll be a master of using AI to polish your prose, identify weaknesses in your story structure, and transform your drafts from good to gleaming. So, grab your metaphorical pen and notebook, and get ready to embark on a journey of editing and polishing fueled by the power of AI! Together, you and your AI partner can turn your creative vision into a masterpiece that will leave your readers breathless.

AI FOR CREATIVES

AI FOR CREATIVES

CHAPTER 9

Escape the Tyranny of the To-Do List:
How AI Can Be Your Productivity Pixie Dust

Feeling like your to-do list is a monstrous hydra, each completed task replaced by two more fearsome chores? Do you dream of escaping the soul-sucking vortex of emails, scheduling nightmares, and administrative tasks, only to find yourself sucked back in the next day? Fear not, fellow creatives! In this chapter, we'll unveil AI, your secret weapon for transforming from a to-do list martyr into a time management master. Think of it as sprinkling productivity pixie dust on your workflow, watching as the chaos transforms into a symphony of streamlined efficiency.

AI, Your Time-Suck Slayer:
- **The Email Assassin:** Does your inbox resemble a digital black hole, swallowing your time and attention whole? Let AI be your email samurai, wielding a digital katana and cleaving through your inbox with laser focus! We'll show you how to use AI to filter out unimportant emails like promotional offers or social media notifications, categorize messages by priority, and even draft concise responses based on pre-set templates. Imagine AI as your tireless email assistant, ensuring only the most important messages reach your attention. No more endless scrolling and

AI FOR CREATIVES

inbox dread – AI becomes your email guardian, freeing you to focus on the creative work that truly matters, whether it's crafting the perfect sentence or composing a heart-wrenching melody.

- **The Scheduling Sorcerer:** Is scheduling meetings and appointments a chaotic juggling act that leaves you feeling like a clown on a unicycle, perpetually on the verge of dropping everything? Let AI be your scheduling sorcerer! We'll explore how to use AI to find the perfect time slots for everyone involved, automatically send invites with clear agendas, and even reschedule conflicts with a single click. Imagine having a digital scheduling whiz at your side, who can navigate the complexities of everyone's calendars and ensure your meetings run smoothly and efficiently. No more wasted time playing email tag or phone Tetris – AI becomes your scheduling guru, freeing you to focus on the creative collaborations that fuel your artistic journey.

AI, Your Repetitive Task Robot:
- **The Data Entry Drudge Destroyer:** Are you bogged down by repetitive data entry tasks that suck the joy out of your creative process, like filling out endless forms or copying and pasting information? Let AI be your data entry robot! We'll show you how to use AI to automate these tedious tasks, freeing you to unleash your creative

spirit on more inspiring endeavors. Imagine AI as your tireless digital assistant, handling the mundane tasks that drain your energy, like updating spreadsheets or generating reports based on your data. No more mind-numbing form completion – AI becomes your administrative automaton, ensuring your workflow stays organized and efficient, leaving you with more time to explore your creative vision.

- **The Research Rabbit Hole Rescuer:** Do you find yourself spending hours lost in research rabbit holes, chasing down information that seems to multiply with each click, only to emerge blinking and bewildered with a sense of accomplishment that quickly fades? Let AI be your research rabbit hole rescuer! We'll delve into using AI to gather relevant information from various sources, summarize key points with crystal clarity, and even anticipate your research needs before you even know you have them. Imagine having a digital research assistant who can navigate the vast ocean of information with lightning speed, surfacing the most valuable nuggets of knowledge and saving you precious time for creative exploration. No more information overload – AI becomes your research sherpa, guiding you through the research labyrinth and ensuring you have the knowledge you need to fuel your creative fire.

AI FOR CREATIVES

Remember, AI isn't here to replace your hustle or creativity; it's here to give you your time back. By the end of this chapter, you'll be a master of using AI to streamline tasks, automate repetitive work, and finally escape the tyranny of the to-do list. So, grab your metaphorical paintbrush, musical instrument, or writer's notebook, and get ready to unleash your creative potential with the help of your AI productivity pixie dust! Let AI become your secret weapon, and watch as you transform from a to-do list warrior into a master of your time and your creative destiny.

AI FOR CREATIVES

AI FOR CREATIVES

CHAPTER 10

AI Apprentices:
How Real-World Creators are Using AI to Forge New Frontiers

We've explored the treasure trove of possibilities that AI offers creatives, but is it all just science fiction? Are artists, musicians, and writers truly wielding this digital magic in their creative endeavors? Buckle up because, in this chapter, we'll crash the workshops and studios of real-world creators who are using AI as their apprentices, pushing the boundaries of their art and defying expectations. Prepare to be inspired by these trailblazers who are forging new creative paths with the help of their AI collaborators.

From Script to Soundscape: How a Sci-Fi Author Used AI to Craft an Immersive Audiobook:
Imagine crafting an audiobook experience that transcends narration, transporting listeners directly into the heart of your sci-fi world. They are no longer passive consumers; they are active participants. That's exactly what author Blake Crouch did for his mind-bending novel "Dark Matter." Instead of a traditional audiobook, Crouch used AI to generate soundscapes that mirrored the emotional tone of each scene. Think sterile hums for the spaceship and unsettling whispers for the alien forest. The result? It is an audiobook experience so immersive that listeners feel like they are characters

themselves, hurtling through the plot twists alongside the protagonist. This innovative collaboration between the author and AI redefined the boundaries of the audiobook format, proving that AI can be a powerful tool for enriching the storytelling experience.

From Sketch to Symphony: How a Pop Star Collaborated with AI to Create a Hit Song:
Sometimes, even the biggest pop stars hit creative roadblocks. Enter Grimes, the genre-bending musician who used AI to co-write her song "Flesh Without Blood." Imagine her frustration – a blank page, a melody stuck in her head, and the pressure to deliver a chart-topping hit. Instead of waiting for inspiration to strike, Grimes fed AI lyrics and melodies from her existing work. The AI, acting as a kind of digital muse, generated new musical phrases and song structures that surprised and challenged Grimes. The result? A track that pushed the boundaries of her signature sound, showcasing the transformative power of AI collaboration in the music industry. This story highlights how AI can be more than just a tool – it can be a creative partner, sparking unexpected ideas and propelling artists to new sonic territories.

From Historical Research to Heartfelt Fiction: How a Historical Novelist Used AI to Breathe Life into Forgotten Characters:
Crafting historical fiction requires meticulous research, but breathing life into characters from a bygone era can be a daunting task. Imagine the challenge – sifting

through dusty archives, deciphering faded letters, and trying to understand the daily lives of people who lived centuries ago. Enter author E.K. Johnston used AI to analyze historical documents and letters to understand the language, slang, and everyday concerns of people from the time period she was writing about. This AI-powered research helped her create characters that felt authentic and relatable, even centuries later. Johnston's characters weren't just historical figures on a page – they were people with hopes, dreams, and anxieties that resonated with readers in the present day. This story exemplifies how AI can be an invaluable research assistant, helping authors bridge the gap between historical fact and fictional narrative.

These are just a few examples of how creatives are wielding AI as their secret weapon. As AI continues to evolve, the possibilities for artistic collaboration are truly limitless. Imagine sculpting a fantastical creature with AI, its movements guided by real-world physics simulations. Or composing a piece of music that adapts to the mood of the audience in real time. The future of creativity is wide open, and AI is poised to be a powerful tool for the next generation of artists, musicians, and writers. This future promises to be a fascinating dance between human imagination and machine intelligence, where the boundaries between creator and collaborator will continue to blur, leading to a renaissance of artistic expression.

AI FOR CREATIVES

CHAPTER 11

The Robot Muse and the Human Artist: A Look at the Creative Future

We've unveiled the exciting potential of AI as a creative partner, but what does the future hold for this dynamic duo? Buckle up, fellow innovators, because we're about to embark on a journey to a future where creativity takes on a whole new meaning. Here, the lines between human and machine will blur, birthing a renaissance of artistic expression unlike anything we've ever witnessed.

The Rise of the Co-Created Canvas:
Imagine a world where artists and AI collaborate on a massive digital canvas, each brushstroke a conversation between human vision and machine ingenuity. Take, for instance, a project like Google's Magenta https://artsandculture.google.com/, where AI algorithms learn from the styles of famous artists like Van Gogh or Monet. Now, envision an artist using a similar interface, feeding the AI their own artistic style and preferred color palettes. The AI might sketch a fantastical landscape based on the artist's emotional state, perhaps a dreamscape filled with floating islands and impossible waterfalls. The artist then steps in, breathing life into it with vibrant colors and intricate details, meticulously crafting a fantastical creature perched on a rock formation. This co-creation could lead to artistic expressions that transcend the boundaries of

individual styles, birthing entirely new aesthetics and pushing the envelope of what art can be.

The Symphony Composed in Real-Time:
Imagine a concert hall where the music adapts to the mood of the audience. Sensors pick up on the collective emotional energy of the room, feeding the information to an AI conductor who guides a virtual orchestra in real time. The music might start out peaceful and serene with gentle cello melodies as the audience settles in. But as the energy intensifies, the AI conductor might introduce driving percussion and soaring violin lines, creating a thrilling crescendo that mirrors the excitement of the crowd. This interactive experience would blur the lines between performer and audience, creating a truly immersive and dynamic musical journey. Imagine attending a concert by your favorite artist, but instead of a pre-rehearsed setlist, the music unfolds based on the collective energy of the audience, becoming a unique experience every single time.

The AI Muse That Dreams in Code:
Imagine a world where writers don't face the dreaded blank page. Instead, they have an AI muse at their side, a digital dream weaver that conjures up story ideas, character sketches, and even plot twists based on the writer's preferences. Perhaps a writer struggling with a new novel could feed the AI details about their desired genre and thematic elements. The AI, acting as a kind of digital brainstorming partner, might generate a series of potential plot hooks, character backstories, and even

evocative snippets of dialogue. This wouldn't replace the human touch, of course. The writer would still be the architect, shaping the raw material provided by AI into a compelling narrative. But with AI as a brainstorming partner, writer's block could become a relic of the past.

The AI Storyteller:
Imagine AI not just as a brainstorming tool but as a collaborator in the storytelling process itself. While some might fear a future where AI writes entire novels, a more likely scenario is a future where AI and human writers work together. The human writer might craft the overall story arc and develop the core characters, while the AI handles the heavy lifting of generating dialogue variations, exploring different narrative branches, and even creating detailed descriptions of fantastical settings. This collaborative approach could streamline the writing process, allowing authors to focus on the emotional core of their stories while AI takes care of the world-building and narrative logistics.

The Human-Machine Tango: A Collaboration, Not a Competition:
As AI continues to evolve, some might fear a future where machines replace human creativity altogether. But the future we envision is one of collaboration, not competition. AI can be a powerful tool, but it lacks the spark of human imagination, the emotional depth, and the lived experiences that shape our creative vision. The future of creativity lies in the harmonious dance between

AI FOR CREATIVES

humans and machines, where AI amplifies our strengths and pushes us to explore new artistic frontiers.

The journey alongside AI promises to be an exciting one, filled with unexpected discoveries and groundbreaking creations. So, grab your metaphorical paintbrush, musical instrument, or writer's notebook, and get ready to co-create the future of art with your AI partner. The possibilities are truly endless, and the only limit is your imagination.

AI FOR CREATIVES

AI FOR CREATIVES

CHAPTER 12

The Art of Balance: Navigating the Ethical Tightrope with AI

So, you're ready to embrace AI as your creative partner? Fantastic! But hold on a minute, intrepid artist. Before we dive headfirst into this exciting new frontier, let's take a moment to consider the ethical landscape. As with any powerful tool, AI comes with its own set of challenges. Imagine wielding a paintbrush that can create masterpieces but also has a hidden bias for a particular color palette, making it impossible to paint a character with realistic skin tones! We need to ensure our AI partners are ethical collaborators, not secret saboteurs of our creative vision.

The Bias in the Brushstrokes:
AI algorithms are only as good as the data they're trained on. And guess what? Data can be riddled with biases, reflecting the prejudices of the real world. Imagine using an AI image generator to create a diverse cast of characters for your graphic novel, only to end up with a group that reinforces stereotypical gender roles or perpetuates outdated beauty standards. Yikes! To avoid such pitfalls, we need to be responsible stewards of AI, carefully evaluating the data sets used to train our AI partners and actively seeking diverse datasets that reflect the rich tapestry of human experience.

AI FOR CREATIVES

For example, if you're a fashion designer using AI to generate new clothing ideas, you might want to ensure the training data includes a wide range of body types, ethnicities, and gender identities. This will help to mitigate bias and ensure your AI partner can create designs that are inclusive and celebrate diversity.

Transparency over Alchemy:
Sometimes, AI feels like a magic black box – you feed it something, and it outpops a creative solution. But what's happening inside that box? This lack of transparency can be a concern, especially when it comes to creative ownership. Imagine a musician collaborating with an AI to write a song, but then the AI takes all the credit! To ensure fair play, we need to develop clear ethical guidelines for AI-assisted creativity. Who owns the rights to a creation – the human artist, the AI, or perhaps a new kind of collaborative entity?

The Human Touch: A Vital Ingredient:
AI shouldn't replace human creativity – it should enhance it. Imagine a world where every novel reads the same, churned out by a formulaic AI program. Bleh! The human touch is what breathes life into art, what infuses it with emotion, vulnerability, and that certain je ne sais quoi. So, let's not get carried away by the allure of AI. While AI can be a powerful tool for generating ideas and streamlining processes, the human element remains irreplaceable.

AI FOR CREATIVES

For instance, a filmmaker might use AI to generate special effects for their movie, but it's the human director who decides how those effects are used to tell the story and evoke emotions in the audience. The human touch is what separates a visually impressive but soulless spectacle from a truly moving cinematic experience.

By approaching AI with a critical eye and a commitment to responsible practices, we can ensure that this powerful tool empowers creativity, fosters diversity, and ushers in a new era of artistic expression. Remember, AI is here to be our partner in crime, not an overlord dictating the future of art. So, let's wield it wisely, ethically, and with a healthy dose of artistic integrity. Now, go forth and create something amazing with your trusty AI sidekick by your side!

AI FOR CREATIVES

CONCLUSION

AI and Creativity: The Encore - A Curtain Call and a Standing Ovation

Bravo! You've reached the final curtain call of this exploration into the fascinating world of AI and creativity. Before we give ourselves a well-deserved round of applause, let's take a moment to bask in the afterglow of the key takeaways and the exciting possibilities that lie ahead.

AI, Your Creative Power-Up Pack:
Remember that feeling of being bogged down by mundane tasks, like drowning in an overflowing inbox or wrestling with a chaotic calendar? We've unveiled AI as your very own creative power-up pack! Imagine the email assassin slicing through your inbox like a digital samurai, freeing you from the tyranny of the to-do list. Or picture the scheduling sorcerer banishing the stress of calendar juggling, ensuring your time is spent on what truly matters – unleashing your creative spirit.

Beyond the Rabbit Hole: Co-Creating Masterpieces:
We've journeyed into the workshops of trailblazing creators who are using AI not as a replacement but as their artistic apprentice. Remember the sci-fi author crafting an immersive audiobook experience that transports listeners to the heart of their fictional world, thanks to AI-generated soundscapes? Or the pop star

who pushed the boundaries of their music by co-writing a song with a digital muse? These are just glimpses into the boundless potential for collaboration, where AI can be the spark that ignites groundbreaking artistic expression. Imagine sculpting a fantastical creature with AI, its movements guided by real-world physics simulations, or composing a piece of music that adapts to the mood of the audience in real time. The future of creativity is a symphony of human imagination and machine intelligence.

A Collaboration, Not a Competition:
Let's dispel any fears of AI taking over the creative landscape. The future we envision isn't one of human versus machine but a harmonious collaboration. AI lacks the spark of human ingenuity, the emotional depth, and the lived experiences that shape our unique creative vision. But with AI amplifying our strengths and pushing us to explore new artistic frontiers, the possibilities become truly limitless.

The Ethical Stage Manager: Setting the Scene for Responsible Creation:
As with any powerful tool, AI requires a responsible approach. Remember, we discussed the importance of being mindful of potential biases in AI algorithms. Imagine a fashion designer using AI to create clothing patterns, only to find the designs unintentionally perpetuate outdated beauty standards. By carefully evaluating the data sets used to train AI and fostering

ethical practices, we can ensure our digital partners enhance, not hinder, our creative expression.

The Encore Performance: A Canvas Awaits

So, dear creative, the stage is yours! Grab your metaphorical paintbrush, musical instrument, or writer's notebook. The future of creativity beckons, a vast canvas waiting to be co-created with your trusty AI partner. With a critical eye, a commitment to responsible practices, and a whole lot of imagination, we can usher in a new era of artistic expression. The only limit is your creativity, and with AI by your side, that limit just vanished into the wings. Now, go forth and create something amazing! The world awaits your unique voice, amplified by the power of AI. This is your encore performance, and we can't wait to see the masterpiece you create.

AI FOR CREATIVES

AI and Creativity: Act III - A Brighter Tomorrow for the Arts

The curtain has closed on this exploration of AI and creativity, but the real performance is just beginning. Imagine the future of art not as a solitary act but as a dazzling theatrical production – a vibrant collaboration between human vision and machine ingenuity. Let's take a final bow and celebrate the optimistic outlook that awaits the creative industries.

From Sidekick to Spotlight: AI, the Creative Collaborator

AI is poised to become more than just a helpful sidekick; it's evolving into a powerful collaborator. Imagine a world where novelists don't face writer's block but brainstorm alongside AI muses that conjure up captivating plot twists and character backstories. Picture fashion designers using AI to create clothing that transcends cultural boundaries, catering to a diverse range of body types and styles. The human touch will always be irreplaceable, but with AI as a co-creator, the wellspring of inspiration will flow more freely than ever before.

Breaking Down the Gates: Democratizing Creativity

AI has the potential to democratize creativity, making artistic expression more accessible. Imagine a world where aspiring musicians can use AI to create professional-sounding compositions, even without years of formal training. Or picture a young filmmaker crafting visually stunning special effects for their movie, powered by user-friendly AI tools. AI can break down the barriers to entry, empowering a new generation of creators to tell their stories and share their unique visions with the world.

A Renaissance of Artistic Expression:
The future of creativity promises to be a renaissance unlike anything we've ever witnessed. Imagine a world where artists and AI co-create fantastical creatures that leap from the pages of books and bound across movie screens. Or picture musicians composing symphonies that adapt to the emotions of the audience in real-time, creating a truly immersive and interactive experience. The boundaries between artistic disciplines will blur, leading to a fusion of art forms that will redefine what creativity can be.

A Symphony of Progress: Humans and Machines in Harmony
This optimistic future isn't about humans being replaced by machines. It's about a harmonious collaboration, a symphony of progress where human and machine play their parts to create something truly magnificent. AI can handle the heavy lifting, freeing us to focus on the emotional core of our work, the vulnerability, and the spark of human imagination that makes art truly resonate.

So, let's embrace AI with open arms, not with fear. Let's see it not as a competitor, but as a powerful tool waiting to be wielded. Together, we can create a future where art

AI FOR CREATIVES

flourishes, where creativity is accessible to all, and where the possibilities are truly limitless. The curtain rises on a new act in human creativity, and it's going to be an incredible show.

AI FOR CREATIVES

AI FOR CREATIVES

APPENDIX

AI Playground: A Curated Toolbox for Creative Minds

AI is no longer a futuristic fantasy; it's a toolbox brimming with potential for artists, musicians, and writers. Here's a glimpse into some exciting AI tools waiting to be explored:

For the Visually Adept:
- **Midjourney https://www.midjourney.com/**: Unleash your inner Salvador Dalí with Midjourney, a powerful AI image generation tool. Feed it text descriptions, and watch as it conjures up fantastical visuals that will ignite your imagination.

- **Nightcafe Creator https://creator.nightcafe.studio/**: Feeling artistic but lacking the technical skills? Nightcafe Creator is your AI muse. Upload your own photos or choose from a library of images, and let AI transform them into stunning works of art in various artistic styles.

- **GauGAN2 https://www.nvidia.com/en-us/research/ai-playground/**: Ever dreamed of painting landscapes like Bob Ross? GauGAN2, created by Google AI, allows you to do just that! Sketch a simple landscape outline, and watch as

AI FOR CREATIVES

AI fills it in with lush greenery, majestic mountains, or even whimsical castles based on your chosen artistic style.

For the Musically Inclined:

- **Amper Music https://ampermusic.zendesk.com/hc/en-us**: Break free from writer's block with Amper Music. This AI-powered tool helps you compose original music by providing melodic inspiration, generating variations on your ideas, and even crafting entire song sections based on your chosen genre.

- **Jukebox https://openai.com/research/jukebox**: Want to collaborate with musical legends? Jukebox, from OpenAI, lets you do just that (sort of). Enter a snippet of music from a particular artist or genre, and Jukebox will continue the composition in that style, creating new and surprising musical journeys.

- **LANDR https://www.landr.com/**: Mastering your music can be a daunting task. LANDR takes the guesswork out of the process with its AI-powered mastering tools. Upload your track, and LANDR will analyze and enhance it, ensuring it sounds polished and professional.

For the Wordsmiths:

AI FOR CREATIVES

- **Jasper** https://www.jasper.ai/: Beat writer's block and overcome creative roadblocks with Jasper, an AI writing assistant. Provide Jasper with a few details about your desired content, and it will generate creative text formats, from blog posts and marketing copy to social media captions and even scripts.

- **WordHero** www.wordhero.co: is an AI writing software tool for writers and marketers.

- **Wordtune** https://www.wordtune.com/: Struggling to find the perfect phrasing? Wordtune uses AI to rewrite your sentences, suggest synonyms, and improve the overall clarity and flow of your writing.

- **Hyperwrite** www.hyperwriteai.com: is an AI writing software tool for writers and marketers.

- **WordPlay** – www.wordplay.ai: AI Article writer and bulk article generator.

- **Grammarly** www.grammarly.com: An AI-powered editor and writing assistant.

This is just a taste of the ever-evolving AI landscape for creatives. With a little exploration, you're sure to find the perfect AI tool to spark your creativity and propel your artistic journey to new heights. Remember, AI is here to empower you, not replace you. So, grab your tools, human and digital, and get ready to create something amazing!

AI FOR CREATIVES

AI FOR CREATIVES

AI FOR CREATIVES

AI FOR CREATIVES

THANK YOU FOR READING

PLEASE LEAVE A REVIEW

AI FOR CREATIVES

AI FOR CREATIVES

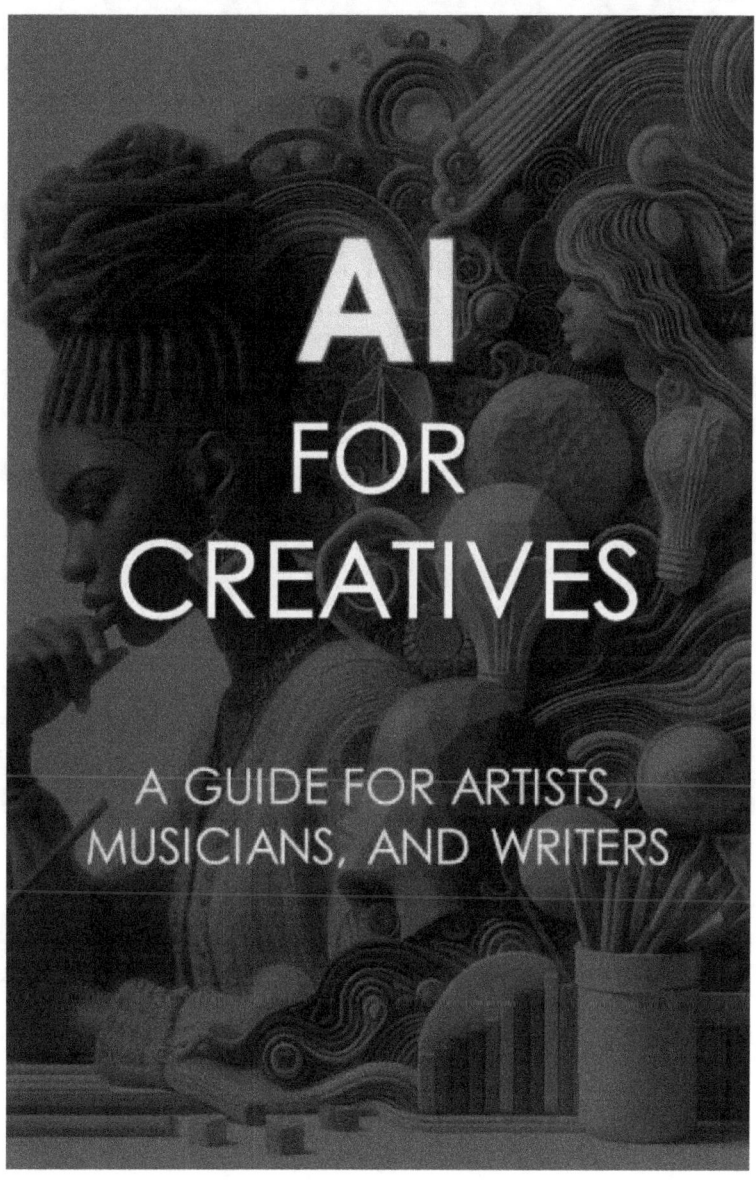

www.ingramcontent.com/pod-product-compliance
Lightning Source LLC
Chambersburg PA
CBHW050328230526
45471CB00005B/2394